Teenage Refugees From

HAITI

Speak Out

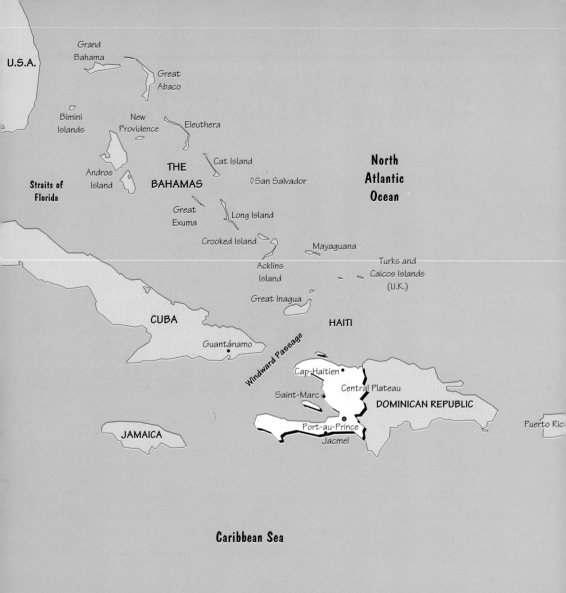

U.S.A.

Grand
Bahama

Great
Abaco

Bimini
Islands

New
Providence

Eleuthera

THE
BAHAMAS

Cat Island

San Salvador

North
Atlantic
Ocean

Straits of
Florida

Andros
Island

Great
Exuma

Long Island

Crooked Island

Mayaguana

Acklins
Island

Turks and
Caicos Islands
(U.K.)

Great Inagua

CUBA

Guantánamo

Windward Passage

HAITI

Cap-Haitien

Central Plateau

Saint-Marc

DOMINICAN REPUBLIC

Puerto Rico

JAMAICA

Port-au-Prince

Jacmel

Caribbean Sea

Netherlands Antilles
(NETH.)

Aruba

Curacao

Bonaire

COLOMBIA

Colon

Panama Canal

Panama

La Palma

IN THEIR OWN VOICES

Teenage Refugees From

HAITI

Speak Out

VALERIE TEKAVEC

M012165205

THE ROSEN PUBLISHING GROUP, INC.
NEW YORK

Published in 1995 by The Rosen Publishing Group, Inc.
29 East 21st Street, New York, NY 10010

First Edition
Copyright © 1995 by The Rosen Publishing Group, Inc.

Manufactured in the United States of America.

Library of Congress Cataloging-in-Publication Data

Teenage refugees from Haiti speak out / [compiled by] Valerie Tekavec. —
1st ed.
  p.   cm. — (In their own voices)
Includes bibliographical references and index.
ISBN 0-8239-1844-0
1. Haitian American teenagers—Juvenile literature. 2. Refugees—United
States—Juvenile literature. [Haitian Americans. 2. Refugees. 3. Youths'
writings.] I. Tekavec, Valerie. II. Series.
E184.H27T44 1995
305.23'5'0899697294073—dc20   94-40367
                                                                   CIP
                                                                   AC

Contents

More than 14,000 Haitian refugees, such as this young girl, were held at the Guantánamo Naval Base. If not allowed to continue to the U.S., they were sent back to Haiti. Many refugees are still being held at Guantánamo.

INTRODUCTION

Haiti's history is filled with terror, corruption, and exploitation. Violence is a constant presence. Until very recently, the country had been under the power of a long line of abusive rulers. Some of these dictators came from within the Haitian population, but the international community has also contributed to the problem.

The history of oppressive rule began with the slave trade in the 18th century. The first Haitians came from many regions of West Africa. They were brought as slaves by the French, who colonized the western part of the island of Hispaniola. They were then forced to work on coffee and sugar plantations.

In the late 1700s, a slave rebellion was led by black revolutionary leader Toussaint L'Ouverture. In 1804, after a series of wars with France, independence was finally achieved. It was the only successful slave revolt to occur in the Caribbean area.

Following victory, however, the country did not establish a popular government. No unity was

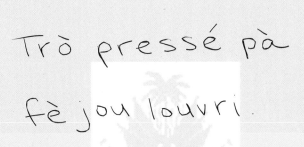

Trò pressé pà fè jou louvri.

ENGLISH TRANSLATION FROM CREOLE:
Rushing does not create the light of day.

achieved, and the economy and agriculture deteriorated. The country had a series of rulers who held power for very short periods of time and offered little vision for the country.

The international community either robbed the country of its resources or excluded it politically with racist policies. Germany, France, and the United States dominated the republic's economy in imports and exports. The Haitians themselves profited very little from their own work and products.

In 1915, the United States military occupied Haiti. World War I was under way and, given the

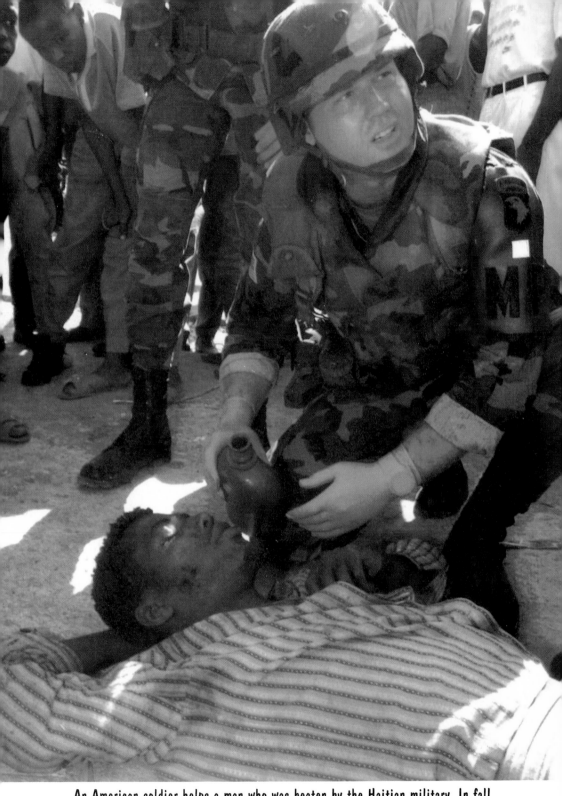

An American soldier helps a man who was beaten by the Haitian military. In fall 1994, U.S. troops arrived in Haiti to assist the transition to democracy.

German presence in Haiti, the United States was interested in securing important strategic locations. The U.S. Navy had long since set up a naval base on the western tip of Cuba at Guantánamo Bay. This gave the U.S. full military control of the important Windward Passage, a sea route into the inner Caribbean and the Panama Canal.

The Americans didn't leave Haiti until 1934. During their 19-year occupation, they did little for the physical condition of the country and ruled arbitrarily over the people, never assisting them with self-rule. Having put most of their energy into training the Haitian military and conducting business and politics with the country's mulatto (mixed Caucasian and African) population, the U.S. left Haiti with a strong military organization and deep racial tension between blacks and mulattos.

After another series of short-lived military dictatorships, one of the most terrible eras of recent Haitian history—the Duvalier dynasty—came about.

François Duvalier, often referred to as "Papa Doc," and his son Jean-Claude, or "Baby Doc," led a corrupt regime of terror that lasted three decades. The regime was infamous for its persecution of those who had hope for the country. François Duvalier created a private militia called the *tonton macoutes,* who carried out random acts of violence, torturing and murdering people who sought peace, equality, and a decent living.

Raoul Cédras, right, led the Haitian military in a violent takeover of the elected government in September 1991. He ruled Haiti until he was forced to leave in October 1994. Emile Jonassaint, left, was sworn in as provisional president.

Jean-Bertrand Aristide, a Catholic priest, became Haiti's first democratically elected president in 1990. He was brought back to govern in 1994 after the 1991 military takeover forced him from office.

While Papa Doc was in power, an exodus, or mass departure, of Haitians to North America took place, robbing the country of its most valuable resource: people. Many of the refugees from the late 1950s to the mid-1980s were professionals in the health, education, and political fields.

Baby Doc did not pose as great a threat to the people as his father had, but the country was traumatized and the military leadership was intact when Baby Doc took control. After thirty years of violence and political corruption, however, the Haitian people had had enough and lashed out violently against Baby Doc and his supporters. Many of the *macoutes* were tortured and killed by mobs in the streets. Baby Doc fled the country.

In December, 1990, Haiti had its first democratic election. The people chose Jean-Bertrand Aristide as their president.

Aristide is a Catholic priest. He has populist political tendencies, which means that he believes in the rights of the common people. He is also very controversial within the Catholic Church. He has many liberal notions of government and religion that have placed him in disfavor with the Church and with conservative political powers around the world. In Haiti, however, he is supported by a vast majority of the people, particularly the poor. In the election of 1990, in which 85 percent of the population participated, Aristide received almost 70 percent of the vote.

Aristide had been in office for only eight months when former Duvalier supporters carried out a coup d'etat. Raoul Cédras, the chief of the Haitian army, and Joseph Michel François, the chief of police, led the violent takeover in September, 1991. Ironically, both men are products of American military training. It is they who are responsible for the most recent atrocities in Haiti.

The new wave of terror and military rule caused another exodus of Haitian refugees. Many attempted to get to the United States.

Both the United States and Canada have sponsored many Haitian refugees. The immigrants have settled in many communities in Florida, New York, Massachusetts, and Quebec.

Leaving Haiti by boat was declared illegal by Haiti's military leaders. A Haitian who tried to do so took many risks. If he was caught, he and his family were imprisoned, beaten, or killed. Many Haitians who decided to run the risk sold most of their possessions to gain passage on a boat. If they ended up being returned to the country by American immigration officials, they came back not only to poverty worse than what they previously had experienced, but to certain abuse from the military. Some of the teenagers in this book took this risk and came to the United States by boat.

The endless abuse of political and human rights has been the cause of profound problems in the

Haitian-American students in Boston listen to President Clinton speak about a potential American invasion of Haiti in September 1994.

economy, education, agriculture, and public health. Haiti is the poorest country in the western hemisphere. Many of the statistics on health and education are comparable to those in some of the most underdeveloped countries in the world. Its cities are known for their slums, like Cité Soleil in Port-au-Prince, where 10,000 people struggle with bad drinking water, starvation, disease, unemployment, and regular violence from the military.

Although embargoes, particularly of fuel, put some pressure on Cédras and François to negotiate with the United States about the return of President **15**

Haitian refugees play soccer at the refugee camp at Guantánamo Naval Base in Cuba. The refugees wait for their fate to be decided by U.S. immigration officials.

Aristide to office, they also brought the economy to a near standstill.

Desperate Haitians began to take to the seas in rickety boats and rafts. Many perished. American officials picked up those they could and took them to the U.S. naval base at Guantánamo, Cuba, where a tent city was built to accommodate them.

President Bill Clinton decided that invasion of Haiti was the only solution to the impasse. He ordered mobilization of forces for that purpose. In the interim, he sent a consultative mission to Haiti, consisting of former President Jimmy Carter, U.S. Senator Sam Nunn, and former Chairman of the Joint Chiefs of Staff Colin Powell. They won a promise from Cédras that he and his supporters would step down from office by October 15, 1994. They indeed did so, two days early, and were escorted by the U.S. military to exile in Panama.

On October 15 President Aristide was restored to office amid scenes of wild enthusiasm from the Haitian people.

Some of the teenagers interviewed for this book asked that their photographs not be used. In some cases, they have done so in order to protect their relatives who remain in Haiti. In all cases, we have used only the students' first names in order to protect their privacy.♦

Sejou is alone in the United States. His entire family is in Haiti, and he probably won't see them for many years.

Sejou is a very clear-thinking young man. At a young age, he knew he wanted to get out of Haiti to make a different life for himself, but he had to take a big risk to do so.

Many Haitian refugees who leave the country by boat, like Sejou, try to get to Guantánamo Bay, an American naval base on the far eastern tip of Cuba. Many Haitians who arrived in Guantánamo were transported back to Haiti. This is what happened to Sejou's uncle.

1
SEJOU
YOUNGEST ON THE BOAT

My name is Sejou. I'm 17 years old. I left my country when I was 13. I've been living in Ipswich, Massachusetts, for one year. Before that I lived for over two years in Guantánamo Bay, seven months in Mississippi, and later in Medford, Massachusetts. Ipswich is a quiet town. I like it here.

I live in a place called the House of Peace. It is a group household of twelve people, two adults and ten kids. I'm one of the youngest people. The kids are from all over the world: the U.S., Haiti, Africa. Some of the Africans are refugees, like me, so we have something in common.

I left Haiti because people were killing people. The country is very dangerous. I was never threatened by the military, but I just wanted to leave. There was a lot of killing in my town. The military would just walk into your house and kill you, for no reason.

A boat filled with Haitian refugees is intercepted by the U.S. Coast Guard.

I left Haiti by boat. Of 31 people on the boat, I was the youngest. My uncle was on the boat, too, but at Guantánamo Bay he was sent back to Haiti.

I remember arriving at Guantánamo in our boat. One morning we saw a big mountain off in the distance, so we headed the boat in that direction and went to Guantánamo.

Life in the refugee camp was sometimes good, sometimes bad. At times, people got into fights. Sometimes it got crowded. I made many friends there, but I don't know where they are now. Some left before me, some left later.

I'm not sure why the U.S. officials didn't send me back to Haiti. Maybe because I was young; maybe because my interview went well. When I was in the camps, I helped people a lot. I helped other people in the camp, and I helped some Americans who worked at Guantánamo. For example, I helped them cook and clean up, wash the car, a lot of things. When the officials came looking for certain people, they would give me a list of names and I would go and find the people. I got to know a lot of people in the camp that way. I'm still in contact with a woman who works there. I was good to her and she was good to me.

I'd like to go back to Haiti one day, but not now. Maybe in ten or fifteen years. It's too dangerous there now. If it doesn't change, I won't go. It has to change first.◆

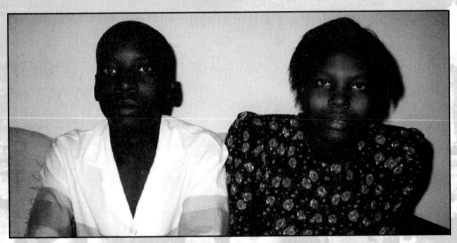

Nicholas and **Vivianne** come from a rural town in Haiti. They grew up under difficult financial conditions that were aggravated because their family was threatened by the military.

When they talk about life in Haiti, there is a sense of relief in their voices, relief in having left, even though they miss it.

NICHOLAS AND VIVIANNE
FAMILY IN DANGER

My name is Nicholas. I'm from Haiti. I came to Jacksonville, Florida, with my family two months ago. I like the United States because it's a different way of life. It's more peaceful here, and I have a chance to go to school, which wasn't possible in Haiti. Now I'm happy; life is completely different for me now.

I come from Gros Morne, a town in the county of Savanne Moulin. It's in the country. The people in the area are very poor. Most of them work the fields.

I never saw any violence in my town, but my family was in great danger. My father was part of a political movement. He was trying to help his countrymen and to fight for what is right. My father was persecuted by the military. We are political refugees. We had to leave because our lives were in danger.

I had friends in Gros Morne. They were sad when I left, but they made me promise to write them and not to forget them. They knew I was leaving for a better life.

I go to school in Jacksonville. I just started. I'm in the tenth grade. I don't speak much English yet, so I'm taking it in school. I'm also taking French. I want to finish school here, study at the university, and become a doctor.

I had problems in Haiti, but I don't have them here any more. I feel free now.

My name is Vivianne. I'm Nicholas' sister. I am 13 years old. I go to school here in Jacksonville. I like it very much. I have made one good friend since I came here, but I only see her at school because we live too far apart.

I love Haiti, but there are a lot of things I didn't have there that I have here. The biggest difference is that in Haiti people were shooting other people a lot. I haven't seen that here yet. I don't feel so afraid any more.

My father was involved in an underground movement in Haiti. The government kept him in jail for some time. We left because of all the repression. After what my parents went through there, maybe we'll have it a little better here.

I still have a lot of family and friends in Haiti. I would like them all to come to the United States

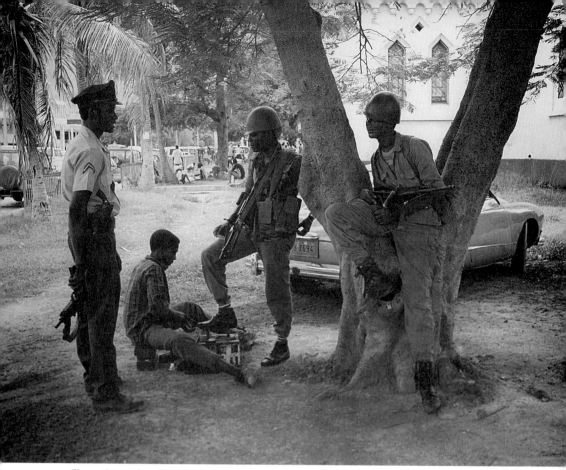

The military has long been a powerful force in Haitian society, at times terrorizing the country's citizens.

because so many people are getting killed there. There are eight people in my family. I have brothers and sisters who are still in Haiti. My parents are trying to bring them here.

My father and mother are learning English now. Once they learn how to speak it, they will be able to find jobs. I would like to be a teacher when I'm older. When there is more democracy in Haiti I would like to go back to visit.◆

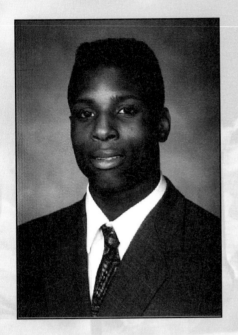

Henri is not new to the United States. He has lived here almost as long as he lived in Haiti. He talks about how difficult it might be to return to Haiti for a long period of time because he is entirely at home in the United States.

HENRI
DEMOCRACY IS NECESSARY

My name is Henri. I've been living in the United States for nine years, since I was eleven. I was born in Croix de Bouquet, a small town about thirty minutes outside of Port-au-Prince. My parents came to the United States before I did. While they were here, I lived with my grandfather. One year later they sent for me. Now I live with my whole family in Huntington Station, New York, on Long Island. I have seven brothers and three sisters.

I haven't been back to Haiti since I left. I haven't had time to go there because I've been very involved in high school wrestling for the past six years. My summers were always busy. I trained a lot, and I went to wrestling camp. As a junior, I was a runner-up in the end of the season competition. As a senior, I took third place. Countywide, I was ranked seventh in my weight class. I also

François Duvalier, also known as "Papa Doc," handed over the leadership of his regime of terror to his son, Jean-Claude, "Baby-Doc" who was forced to flee the country.

played football one year, but wrestling is my favorite sport.

Right now I'm preparing to go to college. I'm still deciding whether I want to go to Farmingdale College, on Long Island, or to Oneonta College, in upstate New York. I might wrestle in college, as an extracurricular activity. I think I'd like to study law.

When I left Haiti, the country was peaceful and calm. The atmosphere was good, and people were getting along. I can't believe what has happened there in recent years. Things started getting out of hand. A lot of people were dying. Fortunately, no one related to me has been hurt.

My fondest memory of Haiti is the lifestyle. For a young person, life there was very stimulating. I studied hard in school, and during vacation I learned new things, like farming. I liked it when the weather was nice, and I liked being with the animals.

Before I left Haiti, my family told me a little bit about what to expect in the U.S. When I first got here, they told me to behave. As far as the adjustment went, I was lucky to be so young. It's easier for young people to make changes. I arrived here on a weekend, and I attended school for the first time the following Monday. The people at my school were great. I had a good ESL teacher. One student, who was Hispanic, showed me around, and we became friends. The community I live in is a mix of ethnic groups. The majority is white, but it's integrated.

Life in the United States gives me the opportunity to do many things. A lot of other countries in the world can't provide those opportunities. I think the most important thing is to follow your dream, or your goal.

Understanding between cultures is important to me, too. I like to circulate with people from all parts of the world. I like knowing about other groups. It's not good to judge others when you don't know anything about them. That's important to me on a personal level, in my friendships. I'm also involved in a Haitian youth group in my community. We meet a lot and have discussions. We have been doing it for two or three years. Every year we put on a multicultural dance festival and all the different groups get together. We try different foods, play music, and stuff like that.

I would like to go back to Haiti someday. I might even go this summer for a couple of weeks. It would be hard to go back to stay for a long time. If I did go, I would probably adjust again, but I don't know what the environment is like now. I don't know if I would feel like I belong there.

My greatest wish for Haiti is that all the violence comes to an end, and that the government is restored. I think democracy is necessary. People need to be educated about democracy. Aristide is a good example for the people. I think he can really help them. He's got what it takes.◆

A young boy wearing the uniform of the Haitian security police takes part in a carnival during the reign of Jean-Claude "Baby Doc" Duvalier.

Sandra was born in Haiti but has spent her adolescence in Canada. She was only six when she and her parents left Haiti. Sandra and her family believe that President Aristide will provide new hope for the people of their country.

SANDRA
SOMETHING HAS TO BE DONE

I was born in Port-au-Prince, Haiti. I lived there with my mother and father. We left Haiti in 1972 because it was difficult for my parents to find work. I was sad to leave my grandparents and cousins. It's a hard thing to leave one's country.

In Haiti I went to school for one year. There we learned to read and write in French and Creole, but at home we most often spoke Creole. Since we live in Quebec, I speak French at home and at school. Although I don't speak much Creole anymore, I can still understand it. My mother still prepares Creole dishes, and we have kept some Haitian traditions. We have continued to practice our faith in a Catholic church in our neighborhood. It is often through the church that new arrivals begin to feel a part of the community.

When we arrived in Canada it was winter time, and that was quite different for me. It took a little time getting used to living in Canada. After all, school was different, the language was different. Even though I spoke French, there were differences in vocabulary and accent that made communicating challenging. When we first arrived we stayed with my aunt. Luckily my parents were able to find work, and we found a place of our own. It was not too long before I was able to make friends and do well at school. The Qúebecois are good people. Currently I'm attending a university and am studying to become a podiatrist.

My favorite memory of Haiti is the Carnival. I remember the music and beautiful colors. I also remember that my bedroom had a big balcony, and I liked that too. I didn't have many friends. I played most of the time with my cousins.

I would like to return to Haiti. It would be nice to see it again, but not right away. My mother, however, does not want to return. She feels that it would be too difficult now with all the violence that goes on.

I wish that the killings and misery in Haiti would end. Something has to be done. My mother thinks that the Americans should do everything they can to help the situation in Haiti, even if it means an invasion. She believes if the United States is capable of helping, they should. We all need one another, after all. My family and I understand why so many Haitians are risking their lives to flee

Two boys fight over a container of milk looted from a store that was set on fire. Food shortages and poverty in Haiti have produced desperation in many people.

their country, but we also realize that the United States can't welcome them all with open arms.

My family's opinion is that the majority of Haitians support Aristide and want him to be their leader. There are some truly bad people who need to be cleared out of there.◆

Claude has been in the United States for two years and is living here alone. He is what relief organizations call an "unaccompanied minor."

Claude must make his way entirely on his own, with the help of organizations who sponsor refugees.

CLAUDE
WITHOUT MY FAMILY

My name is Claude. I'm 19 years old. I come from St. Marc, Haiti, on the coast of the Golfe de la Gonave, north of Port-au-Prince.

I left Haiti two years ago and now live in Ipswich, Massachusetts. It's located about one hour north of Boston, close to the ocean. Ipswich is a nice place. It's a small town, good for studying, because it's so quiet.

I left Haiti when I was 17. At first I lived in Waltham, Massachusetts, where a Catholic church organization sponsored me as a refugee. Then I moved here, where I live in a community of other young refugees.

I go to school in Ipswich. I'm a senior in high school. When I finish, I'd like to go to college in Boston, maybe to Bunker Hill College.

Haitians watch a U.S. warship looming off the coast of Port-au-Prince. The presence of the U.S. military was prominent in Haiti in the fall of 1994.

When I left my country, I went by boat with a group of people. I ended up at Guántanamo Bay. I don't like talking about this time in my life. It was difficult.

When I first got here, everything was very new. I didn't speak English at first, but I had an ESL teacher. That was very helpful. It took some time to adjust to American life. It's hard to live in a new place without your family. My family is still in Haiti. I have five sisters and one brother. Some-

times I get homesick. Lately, it's been difficult to

contact them by phone, because the phone lines are down, but I can still reach them by letter.

I left Haiti because of the military. I didn't want them to get me, so I had to leave. I had to keep on the move. If they catch you, they kill you.

I would like to go back to Haiti someday, but only if things there are cool again. It's not good there right now. My biggest wish for Haiti is that things settle down there. I'd like to finish my education in the U.S. and go back to Haiti, if the situation improves. I'd like to see my family again.

Some American teenagers don't understand my situation. They haven't had to experience what it's like to want peace so much. Some of them only think of the dollar, and that's all they know. They think they know a lot because they live in the United States, but they haven't experienced the kinds of things I have.◆

Guesly is sixteen years old. When he first came to the United States he lived in Miami, Florida. Miami has one of the largest Haitian populations in the country.

Geographically, Florida is very close to Haiti. Only a few miles of water separate the two countries. Guesly now lives in Fort Pierce, Florida.

GUESLY
LIFE CAN BE TOUGH

My name is Guesly. I was born in Cap-Haitien, a large town on the far northern coast of Haiti. I came to Florida almost nine years ago, when I was eight years old. My whole family lives in the United States now. I have two sisters and three brothers, including my twin brother Leslie.

Getting to America was pretty easy. We came by plane, and we didn't have any problems getting the necessary papers. My father came to the United States first, in 1979. He wanted us to grow up in a new land, so, in 1985, he came back to Haiti to get us. Years before that, when he still lived in Haiti, my father was a schoolteacher, but later he became a minister. Now he is a Methodist minister and has his own congregation here in Fort Pierce, Florida.

Leaving Haiti was like going on an exciting journey, because I was on my way to a new land. There were so many things I didn't know about. It was fun. When we first moved here, we lived in Miami. Two years ago, my father was transferred to Fort Pierce, in Saint Lucy County, about two hours out of Miami. I don't like Fort Pierce as much as Miami. Miami was more fun. When we lived down there, I was out with my friends most of the time. We went to the movies, rode go-carts. We always had something to do, all of my brothers and sisters and I. Up here, there's less to do.

I also found school in Miami to be more of a challenge. My sister Sabine feels the same way. Fort Pierce isn't a small town, about 40 to 50 thousand people. It's a lot smaller than Miami. Sabine says it feels like only 100 people live here!

In my free time, I play a lot of soccer. I play on my school team and also for a private team. I've been playing since I was very little. I joined my first club when I was twelve. Basically, I play center mid-field, off left wing. But most of the time the coach uses my twin brother and me as the "liberals"; that means we play almost any position where they need us. Leslie and I both play on the same teams.

My favorite subject in school is medical skills, and I like math and science a lot. I want to go to a Methodist college when I'm finished with high

I don't know a lot about what's going on down in Haiti politically, only what I get from the newspaper. Sometimes a friend or relative writes something to us. As far as Aristide is concerned, I feel that if the international community had been more organized and put their heads together, things in Haiti would have worked out better.

Life in the United States can be tough for some Haitians. It's important to me that American kids treat Haitian kids as equals. A lot of the time American kids make fun of Haitian kids. They really don't bother me and my brother because we get good grades in school. They come to us when they need help. They know that we are smart and that we just won't listen to their stupid talk, that we'll ignore them. But they bother other Haitian kids.◆

Rosie has a very special family. Nearly all nineteen of her brothers and sisters are refugees from Haiti and they all live together in a big house with their adoptive parents in Shelbyville, Indiana. Rosie's parents are missionaries.

7

ROSIE
THEY GUESSED MY AGE

My name is Rosie. I'm 19 years old. I come from Haiti, but I don't remember very much about where I was born. It was somewhere in the mountainous area surrounding the Central Plateau. I don't remember it because Mom and Dad adopted me when I was very little.

I have nine brothers and ten sisters. Seventeen of my siblings came from Haiti. Mom had already had one child in the United States, and she adopted one in Indiana before she and Dad went to Haiti as missionaries. My parents adopted me and many of my siblings while they were living in Haiti.

I don't remember meeting my mother. I was three, four, maybe five years old. They didn't know for sure. There is a lot of sickness and poverty in Haiti, and when they adopted me they had to guess my age.

I don't remember my other parents. I consider Mom and Dad my real parents because I've always lived with them. Being adopted or being black was never a big deal to me, because I was always their child. All my brothers and sisters feel the same way about it. I know because I'm the oldest, and they can't remember anybody but Mom and Dad.

I've been living in Shelbyville, Indiana, for about four months. Before that we lived in North Vernon, about an hour from here. Before that we lived in a little camp area in Greensburg, also in Indiana.

We came to the United States in December 1989. We didn't come directly from Haiti, but from the Dominican Republic. We lived in the Dominican Alps, in a town called Jarabacoa, for two and a half years. We lived there because life in Haiti had become so difficult and dangerous.

I'm a home-schooler. All my brothers and sisters have school at home, too. Dad teaches us, and so does Mom. We also have a big brother. He and his wife teach us, and some volunteers help, too. I don't really have to be in school, because I'm 19, but I'm studying at home to take the GED.

I might get a job grooming dogs. It would be a nice job because I have a way with animals. I have a cat named Jonathan. I taught him a lot of tricks. He can lie down on command, he comes when you call him, and he can even wave good-bye. He's really smart.

Haitians squeeze onto the back of a truck leaving Port-au-Prince. An international trade embargo on Haiti contributed to rising fuel prices.

When I first arrived in the United States it felt very cold to me. Now I'm used to the weather. It was a big change because the weather is always warm in Haiti.

My family and I go to different churches in Shelbyville. We just moved here so we don't know which parish we'll be involved with. Different people have invited us to their churches, so we're trying them all out.

Twenty-eight people live in my house. There are two of us to a bedroom. I think there are eight boys' bedrooms and six girls' rooms. We live in a rural area, about ten minutes from Shelbyville. There are a lot of fields around us.

Mom stays at home with me and my brothers and sisters. Dad works. He has several part-time jobs and is very busy. My parents speak Creole and so do all the kids, but we don't speak it at home very much. We usually speak English. Our big brother knows how to speak Creole, too.

In my free time, I like to cook. I also enjoy reading. My favorite books are Westerns and funny stories. I might like to become a nurse in the future. I would like to take care of people. The important thing that has helped me in my life so far is knowing that God is in control, and when He's in control everything is going to be all right.◆

Two Haitian children who have already been sent back to Haiti once before look for boats to take them away again.

Joslin is sixteen years old. He grew up in Haiti's capital, Port-au-Prince. He's a tough kid and he comes from a tough place.

JOSLIN
AFRAID TO GO BACK

I come from Port-au-Prince, Haiti. I've been living in Jacksonville, Florida, for almost six years. When my family left Haiti, my mama came first, with my two older sisters. Then she sent for the rest of us. I have seven brothers and sisters; two of them were born here. My mama sent for us because there was too much violence in Haiti, too much killing. My father didn't come to the United States with us. He died in Haiti.

I didn't want to leave Port-au-Prince because I had friends there. But now I'm afraid to go back because of the killing. It's worse now than when I left. I've seen stuff on the news that didn't happen when I lived there.

I didn't really see much violence when I was in Haiti, except that my friends and I used to get into trouble all the time. We used to start fights, get into fights. I don't get into much trouble here, unless somebody tries to start trouble with me.

Haitians look on in horror at the body of a man shot by police.

When I got into trouble in Haiti, my older sister would smack me. Every night I'd get punished! My friends used to come to my house and pick me up. Then we would go and hang out. We tried to meet girls. We got into trouble sometimes, fights. you know. My sister didn't like that. She was afraid I'd get into real trouble, so she'd smack me. I just wanted to go outside with my friends. But as soon as I came home, she'd smack me. I did this every day and so did she. My sister is 24 now. She won't smack me anymore. Besides, she can't.

She knows I could smack her right back. I would never do that, but she knows I could.

I never got into anything with the military in Haiti, and I'm glad, because those people don't play. When Jean-Claude Duvalier was in power, they were called *tonton macoutes*. You couldn't even look at one of them, because they had you in check, they had you under control. Anything you did, they would just whip you! But when Duvalier left, they got beaten by the people.

I have good friends here in Jacksonville. They remind me of my friends back in Haiti. One of them came to the U.S. four months ago. He's a new refugee. I didn't know him in Haiti, but he's a lot like one of my best friends there. And I'm hanging out with this bad dude named J.P. He's American. He's as bad as my friends back in Haiti. So I have two good friends here and they remind me a lot of my good friends in Port-au-Prince and my life in Haiti.

I sent my friends in Haiti some money, so they don't think I forgot them. When I start working, I'm going to send some more money. I need to find a job so I can send them at least forty dollars a month, so they can reminisce about me.

I really don't want to go back to Haiti. I like my life here better. It's violent here, too, because of guns, gun shooting, gangsters! But in Haiti you know the police won't do anything to help if you're in trouble, the police are bad people there.

I like the girls here. There's a lot of clubs here where you can dance, you know, and get with the girls. We just hang out around the clubs. They won't let you in if you're not a certain age. We go to the mall sometimes, too, have some fun, watch a movie. Or we go to the game room and hang out. We meet girls there. There are no Haitian girls here to talk to. It would be good if there were some Haitian girls here, too.

My school is near my house. I walk there every day. I'm late every day. School starts at 7:15 in the morning. It's too early! When the school year started, you walked in the darkness just to get there for first period! Now it's better since the clocks were set back, but I'm still late!

I like the food here. In Haiti you eat the same food every day. My mom still cooks Haitian food sometimes, but my little brother and sister don't like it so much. They were born here. In Haiti, it's the same old thing, every day. Rice every day, rice, rice! Every color of rice, black rice, green rice. If you don't eat it for a while it tastes good. But when you eat it every day, it gets boring.

I came here by plane. My mama had to do a lot of stuff before we got on that plane! We had to apply for Social Security, a visa, and an alien card. If you don't have that you really can't do a lot in the United States. She applied for all of us to be refugees. Some people come here without the

Haitian President Jean-Bertrand Aristide gestures to a crowd at the National Palace in Port-au-Prince after returning to power on October 15, 1994.

A Haitian boy carries his younger brother through a refugee camp in Port-au-Prince, where they live after having been deported from the Dominican Republic.

alien card and they can't do too much. If you have the card, you're free, like an American. It took her three years to get all the papers.

I remember leaving Haiti. There's a girl there I used to like; she blew me a kiss at the airport. When I got on the plane I was crying. I didn't want to leave Haiti. And when I got up here it was cold! Down there it's hot all the time. Now I'm used to the weather in Jacksonville.

If I could change something about Haiti, I think I'd rebuild the whole country. Like the streets. The

streets are rough and there's a lot of mud when

you go out of town. I would try to fix that. Bridges, all that stuff. The whole country needs to be rebuilt.

Haiti is a nice place, though. There are a lot of fun, good-looking places. But the news on TV makes me mad. When they show the U.S. somewhere else, they show all the good places, like all the tall buildings. But when Americans take pictures of someone else's country, they only picture the bad part. They go to Haiti and take all those ugly scenes and come here and show it to the United States. And then I look at it and it makes me look bad. And I know there are good-looking places in Haiti. Haiti looks good. It's nice.◆

A Haitian basket-seller stops to watch a U.S. soldier on foot patrol.

Glossary

corrupt Debased in character; given to improper conduct.

coup d'etat The violent ousting of a government by a small group of dissenters.

exodus Mass departure or emigration from a country or region.

exploitation Practice of using others badly for one's own advantage.

mulatto Person of mixed race; having one black and one white parent.

oppression Use of power in an unjust or cruel manner.

persecution Subjection to harsh or cruel treatment because of religion, race, etc.

populist In politics, person claiming to represent the common people.

traumatize To injure physically or psychologically, as by mental cruelty, war, or accident.

For Further Reading

Abbot, Elizabeth. *Haiti: The Duvaliers and Their Legacy.* New York: McGraw Hill, 1988.

Aristide, Jean-Bertrand. *In the Parish of the Poor: Writings from Haiti.* New York: Orbis Books, 1990.

———. *Jean-Bertrand Aristide: An Autobiography.* New York: Orbis Books, 1993.

Dash, J. Michael. *Haiti and the United States: National Stereotypes and the Literary Imagination.* New York: St. Martin's Press, 1988.

Farmer, Paul. *AIDS and Accusation: Haiti and the Geography of Blame.* Berkeley: University of California Press, 1992.

Ferguson, James. *Papa Doc, Baby Doc: Haiti and the Duvaliers.* Oxford, New York: B. Blackwell, 1988.

Gold, Herbert. *Best Nightmare on Earth: A Life in Haiti.* New York: Simon and Schuster, 1991.

Hurston, Zora Neale. *Tell My Horse: Voodoo Life in Haiti and Jamaica.* California: Borgo Press, 1992.

Steber, Maggie. *Dancing on Fire: Photographs from Haiti.* New York: Aperture Foundation, 1991.

Temple, Frances. *Taste of Salt.* New York: Orchard Books, 1992.

Index

ACKNOWLEDGMENTS
Thanks to Jeanne Strazzabosco for additional research.

ABOUT THE AUTHOR
Valerie Tekavec, author of a forthcoming book of short stories, *Peacocks and Beans*, is a freelance writer and translator. She is currently working toward her doctorate in German literature at the City University of New York Graduate Center. She teaches German poetry at Bard, and German language at the State University of New York at New Paltz.
  Ms. Tekavec lives in Woodstock, New York.

PHOTO CREDITS
pp. 22 and 52 © Valerie Tekavec; all other photos © AP/Wide World Photos

LAYOUT AND DESIGN
Kim Sonsky